FAMOUS EXPLORERS OF THE AMERICAN WEST™

JOHN CHARLES FRÉMONT

The Pathfinder

CHARLES W. MAYNARD

The Rosen Publishing Group's
PowerKids Press™
New York

For the Scott Clan—Pat, Sid, Kathy and Greg, Patti and Steve, Josh, Jamie, Sydney, Grandmother Scott, and most of all, Sidney

"In the sight of such a mass of life, the traveler feels a strange emotion of grandeur. We had heard from a distance a dull and confused murmuring, and when we came in view of their [the bisons] *dark masses, there was not one among us who did not feel his heart beat quicker. . . . Indians and buffalo make the poetry and life of the prairie, and our camp was full of their exhilaration."*—John Charles Frémont, upon seeing a great herd of bison while he was on a mapping expedition on the Oregon Trail in July 1842.

Published in 2003 by The Rosen Publishing Group, Inc.
29 East 21st Street, New York, NY 10010

First Edition

Managing Editor: Kathy Kuhtz Campbell
Book Design: Maria E. Melendez

Photo Credits: Cover and title page, p. 4 (bottom) Library of Congress Prints and Photographs Division; pp. 4 (top), 11 (top), 15 (top) © CORBIS; pp. 7, 9, 11 (bottom) © Smithsonian American Art Museum/Washington, DC/Art Resource; p. 8 (top) © Southwest Museum Collection; p. 8 (bottom) Joslyn Art Museum, Omaha; p. 12 (top) © Underwood & Underwood/CORBIS; p.12 (bottom) National Cowboy and Western Heritage Museum; p. 15 (bottom) Maria E. Melendez; p. 16 (left) Society of California Pioneers; p. 16 (right) © Bettmann/CORBIS; p. 17 Daguerreotype Collection, Library of Congress Prints and Photographs Division; p.19 © The Granger Collection; p. 20 © North Wind Picture Archives.

Maynard, Charles W. (Charles William), 1955–
John Charles Frémont : the pathfinder / Charles W. Maynard.— 1st ed.
p. cm. — (Famous explorers of the American West)
Includes bibliographical references and index.
Summary: A brief biography of the man who helped open the way west to California and was later elected as a United States Senator from that state.
ISBN 0-8239-6289-X (lib. bdg.)
1. Frémont, John Charles, 1813–1890—Juvenile literature. 2. Explorers—United States—Biography—Juvenile literature. 3. Explorers—West (U.S.)—Biography—Juvenile literature. 4. West (U.S.)—Discovery and exploration—Juvenile literature. 5. Generals—United States—Biography—Juvenile literature. 6. Presidential candidates—United States—Biography—Juvenile literature. 7. United States—Territorial expansion—Juvenile literature. [1.Frémont, John Charles, 1813–1890. 2. Explorers. 3. West (U.S.)—Discovery and exploration.] I. Title. II. Series.
E415.9.F8 M39 2003

2001006665

Manufactured in the United States of America

CONTENTS

Joel Poinsett, Frémont's supporter, was a congressman from South Carolina, a diplomat to Mexico, and secretary of war for President Martin Van Buren. The poinsettia, a plant Poinsett brought from Mexico to the United States, was named for him.

Right: *In the winter of 1836–37, Frémont (photographed here many years later) helped to map the southern Appalachian Mountains.*

EARLY LIFE

John Charles Frémont was born on January 21, 1813, in Savannah, Georgia. His father, also named John Charles, was from France. Anne Beverley Whiting, John Charles's mother, was the daughter of Colonel Thomas Whiting of Richmond, Virginia. When John Charles was only five years old, his father died. His mother sent him to school in Charleston, South Carolina. He enjoyed studying Greek, Latin, **astronomy**, and **mathematics**. As a young man, Frémont met U.S. **diplomat** Joel Poinsett. In 1833, Poinsett encouraged Frémont to go to South America on the ship *Natchez*. For two years Frémont taught mathematics to the sailors. When he returned to the United States, he went on a **survey** for a railroad to measure the land from Charleston to Cincinnati, Ohio.

FIRST EXPLORATIONS

In 1837, Frémont became a second lieutenant in the U.S. **Topographical Corps**. The Army's Topographical Corps surveyed the country and made maps. The Corps tried to find routes for the building of roads and railroads.

Frémont joined Joseph N. Nicollet's **expedition** to map the upper Mississippi River in 1838. The group carefully surveyed the mighty river and the area of the Minnesota River that Zebulon Pike and others had explored 33 years before.

In 1839, Nicollet led an expedition up the Missouri River. At Fort Pierre, in present-day South Dakota, the group left the Missouri River to cross the wide plains. One day a herd of **bison** appeared. The men, including Frémont, rode horses into the herd to shoot some of the bison for food.

The bison started to run. Frémont rode into the cloud of dust. When the herd passed, he did not see anyone else. He had no idea where his camp was. At sunset he still wandered the plains. In the distance, a rocket arced into the sky. His friends were signaling him from the camp, which was many miles (km) away. He rejoined them the next morning.

Bison are seen here running near the upper Missouri River. The words "buffalo" and "bison" often are used to describe the same animal. The American buffalo is a bison. Frémont hunted bison in 1839.

Left: *Jessie Benton, a daughter of Senator Thomas Hart Benton of Missouri, was a talented young woman and was well known in Washington, D.C. She secretly married Frémont on October 19, 1841.*

In the 1840s, Wyoming's Fort Laramie became an important trading and military post along the Oregon Trail. Frémont's maps of the Oregon Trail helped to encourage travelers to settle the West.

MAPPING THE OREGON TRAIL

After the trips with Nicollet, Frémont worked with Nicollet in Washington, D.C. They drew maps of the Mississippi and Missouri Rivers. While in Washington, Frémont met Jessie Benton, the daughter of Senator Thomas Hart Benton. Frémont married her in 1841.

In 1842, Frémont went west to map the Oregon Trail. On the trip up the Missouri River, he met the **mountain man** Kit Carson and asked Carson to guide him up the Oregon Trail to South Pass in the Rocky Mountains. After reaching South Pass, Frémont went into the Wind River Range. He flew a U.S. flag on the peak that is now called Fremont Peak.

Mountain man Jim Bridger warned Frémont at Fort Laramie about Sioux warriors who were killing people along the Oregon Trail. Frémont pressed on anyway. George Catlin painted The Dog, a Sioux chief (above), in 1832.

THE SECOND EXPEDITION

After Frémont returned to Washington, D.C., from the Wind River Range, Jessie gave birth to the Frémonts' first child, Lily. Frémont did not stay home for long. He led 39 men, including Kit Carson and an African American explorer, Jacob Dodson, west into the Rocky Mountains. In the summer of 1843, they explored the Great Salt Lake and crossed the desert to Oregon. They crossed the Sierra Nevada in midwinter to get to California. The snow that had fallen on the peaks made it hard for them to travel. The sun's reflection on the snow blinded the men. They wore handkerchiefs over their eyes to protect them. In March 1844, the men visited Sutter's Fort, where Sacramento is located today. They returned to the United States through southern California and the Mojave Desert.

Frémont and his companions climbed one of the highest peaks of the Wind River Range in 1842. Frémont is shown planting the U.S. flag at the top of the 13,745-foot (4,189-m) mountain that now bears his name.

Bod-a-sin, chief of the Delaware, appears in this painting from 1830. Among the 39 men who went with Frémont to the Rocky Mountains were some Delaware, Native Americans who lived originally in the Delaware Valley.

Christopher "Kit" Carson guided Frémont in 1842, and would join him on two later expeditions to the Far West.

People used Frémont's reports and maps as guidebooks to the Oregon Trail (pictured above in an 1869 painting). Frémont and his scout Kit Carson became well known for their explorations.

Each time Frémont came home, he wrote a report about the expedition on which he had just gone. His wife, Jessie, helped him write all about the West. Many people read these books by the Frémonts and decided to move west to live in Oregon and California. Frémont wrote about the rich soil of the Great Plains. These writings helped Americans learn about the West and the possibilities of living there. People eagerly read about Frémont's adventures. They called Frémont the Pathfinder, because he showed the way to Great Salt Lake, California, and Oregon. In his writings, he suggested names for places that he observed, and these names are still in use today. Nebraska, the Great Basin, and Golden Gate Harbor owe their names to John Charles Frémont.

THE THIRD EXPEDITION

In August 1845, Frémont and Carson left Bent's Fort, in Colorado, with 60 men to go to California on a third expedition. The men crossed the Rockies, the Great Basin, and the Sierra Nevada into California. The Mexicans were afraid Frémont and his men would try to take California from them. Frémont decided to leave California to take his men to Klamath Lake in Oregon. At the lake, Klamath warriors attacked Frémont's camp in the night. Carson heard a noise and shouted an alarm. In the fighting, Frémont and his horse, Sacramento, knocked down a Klamath who was taking aim at Carson. Frémont saved Carson's life, but three men died in the battle. Frémont then moved his men back to California to help the United States if a war with Mexico began.

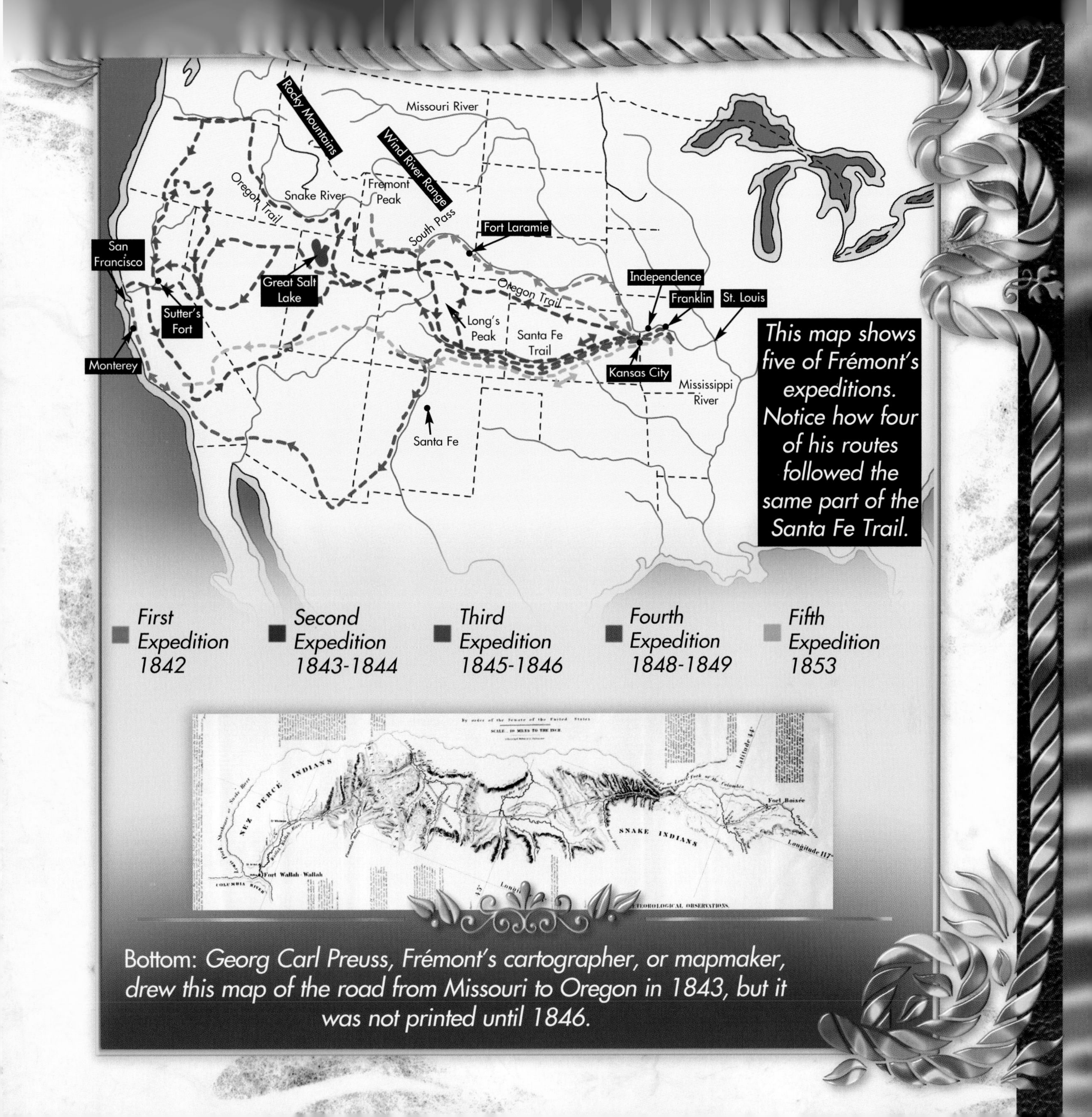

This map shows five of Frémont's expeditions. Notice how four of his routes followed the same part of the Santa Fe Trail.

Bottom: *Georg Carl Preuss, Frémont's cartographer, or mapmaker, drew this map of the road from Missouri to Oregon in 1843, but it was not printed until 1846.*

Above: *The settlers in California who fought against the Mexican government made their own flag, which pictured a bear. These settlers called themselves Osos, which is the Spanish word for "bears."*

Right: *Commodore Robert F. Stockton of the U.S. Navy made Frémont a major and gave him command of the California volunteers. Frémont worked with Stockton to keep California for the United States.*

THE BEAR FLAG REVOLT

As Frémont and his men arrived in California, American settlers **revolted** against the Mexicans who ruled California. These settlers made a flag with a picture of a grizzly bear to show their fighting spirit. Mexican general Mariano Vallejo **surrendered** to a small army of settlers at Sonoma, California, in June 1846. Frémont claimed California for the United States, but the war was not finished. The **Mexican War** (1846–1848) took place mostly in Mexico. In December 1846, General Stephen Kearny brought more U.S. troops to California. Kearny ordered Frémont to go back to Washington.

Senator Thomas Hart Benton supported his son-in-law's journeys to the West. Benton believed in Manifest Destiny. People with this view claimed that it was the United States's right to settle the entire continent, from the Atlantic Ocean to the Pacific Ocean.

RAILROAD SURVEYS

As the United States grew from the Atlantic Ocean to the Pacific Ocean, the country needed railroads to link the East with the West. In 1848, Frémont led another expedition to survey a route for a railroad from the upper Rio Grande to California. He tried to find a route through the Rocky Mountains that could be used even in the winter. Frémont and his men struggled through the deep snow. Mules and horses froze to death in the bitter cold. Eleven of Frémont's 33 men died in the snowy mountains. He and the rest of his men withdrew to New Mexico after failing in their mission.

In 1853, Frémont tried again to survey a route for a railroad through the Rockies. Twenty-two men went with Frémont through the snowy mountains. Food ran low. The hungry, cold men pushed on, eating horse and mule meat. One man froze to death while riding his horse. Still, this expedition proved to be a success. This time Frémont's group reached California, showing that a railroad could be built through the high Rocky Mountains.

A picture from 1875 shows the laying of railroad tracks on the Great Plains. Frémont made maps of routes of possible railroads from St. Louis to the Bay of San Francisco in 1849.

Frémont served as governor of the Arizona Territory from 1878–1883. This illustration shows Frémont as he looked during his later years.

TIMELINE

1813 *On January 21, John Charles Frémont is born in Savannah, Georgia.*

1818 *Frémont's father dies.*

1833 *Frémont sails to South America.*

1837–38 *He goes to the upper Mississippi River with Joseph Nicollet.*

1838–39 *Nicollet and Frémont go on an expedition on the Missouri River.*

1841 *On October 19, Frémont marries Jessie Benton.*

1842 *On June 10, Frémont begins his first expedition to South Pass.*

1843 *On May 29, he begins his second expedition, to Oregon and California.*

1845–47 *Frémont conducts his third expedition, to California.*

1845 *The Bear Flag Revolt in California begins.*

1848 *Frémont leads his fourth expedition.*

1850 *He is elected to the U.S. Senate from California.*

1853 *He goes to California on his fifth expedition.*

1856 *He is the new Republican party's candidate for U.S. president.*

1861 *President Abraham Lincoln names Frémont a major general.*

1890 *On July 13, Frémont dies.*

FRÉMONT'S GOLD

Through the work of Frémont and others, California finally became a part of the United States in 1850. In 1848, gold was discovered at Sutter's Mill near the American River in California. Frémont was connected to California in many ways. He mapped the routes to California for trails, roads, and railroads. In the late 1840s, he built an **estate** in Bear Valley that he called Mariposa, after the mariposa lily. Frémont and his family lived at Mariposa. When gold was discovered at Mariposa, he became a millionaire.

Frémont tried to use his money to build railroads to the West, but he lost most of it. His wife, Jessie, wrote books and articles to support the Frémonts in their later years. On July 13, 1890, John Charles Frémont died.

CITIES FROM ASHES

Frémont achieved many other goals in his long life. California elected him to be one of its first U.S. senators in 1850. In 1856, the new Republican party chose Frémont to run for the office of president of the United States. He lost the election to James Buchanan.

During the **Civil War** (1861–1865), Frémont served as a major general in the army until 1863. After the war he tried to build railroads, and he gave lectures. He also tried to write books.

Frémont's work as the Pathfinder had showed the best places to build roads, cities, and railroads. His wife, Jessie, once said, " . . . from the ashes of his campfires have sprung cities." Frémont's routes, books, and maps helped Americans move west to make the United States what it is today.

GLOSSARY

astronomy (uh-STRAH-nuh-mee) The science of the Sun, the Moon, the planets, and the stars.

bison (BY-sun) A large, four-legged creature, often called a buffalo, that has shaggy fur and is found on the Great Plains.

Civil War (SIH-vul WOR) A war between two sides within one country. America's Civil War was fought in the United States between the Union (northern states) and the Confederacy (southern states) between 1861–1865.

diplomat (DIH-pluh-mat) A person whose job is to handle relations between his or her country and other countries.

estate (is-TAYT) A large piece of land that might have a large house built on it.

expedition (ek-spuh-DIH-shun) A trip for a special purpose, such as scientific study or exploration.

mathematics (math-MA-tiks) The study of numbers.

Mexican War (MEK-sih-kan WOR) The war between the United States and Mexico fought between 1846 and 1848.

mountain man (MOWN-tun MAN) A man who hunted beavers in the Rocky Mountains in the early 1800s.

revolted (rih-VOLT-ed) To have fought or rebelled against a government or other authority.

surrendered (suh-REN-derd) To have given up.

survey (SER-vay) A measuring of land.

Topographical Corps (tah-puh-GRA-fih-kul KOR) A part of the U.S. Army that measured and mapped the country.

INDEX

PRIMARY SOURCES

Cover and Page 1. *John Charles Frémont.* In 1850, Francis D'Avignon made this lithograph for a series that was based on Mathew Brady's portraits of famous heroes of that time. **Page 4 (left).** *The Secretary of War Presenting a Stand of Colors to the 1st Regiment of Republican Bloodhounds.* This is a silhouetted detail from a political cartoon probably drawn by Napoleon Sarony (who signed the work Bow Wow-Wow) in 1840. **Page 7.** *Buffalo Bulls Fighting in Running Season, Upper Missouri.* Artist George Catlin painted this picture sometime between 1837 and 1839. Catlin visited the West from 1830 to 1836 and is famous today for his portraits and sketches of Native Americans and Native American life. This painting is in the Smithsonian American Art Museum. **Page 8 (left).** *Jessie Benton Frémont.* T. Buchanan Read painted this portrait of Frémont's wife, Jessie, in 1856. **Page 8 (bottom).** *Fort Laramie.* Alfred Jacob Miller provided the only visual record of the first Fort Laramie, erected in 1834. Situated in eastern Wyoming, Fort Laramie was an important stop for travelers on the Oregon Trail. **Page 9.** *The Dog, Chief of the Bad Arrow Points Band.* George Catlin painted this portrait of the Sioux chief in 1832, and it is now in The National Museum of American Art, The Smithsonian Institution, Washington, D.C. **Page 11 (bottom).** *Bod-a-sin, Chief of the Tribe.* Delaware chief Bod-a-sin's portrait was painted by George Catlin in 1830. Even at this time, the Delaware had started to wear white people's clothing as part of their dress. **Page 12 (bottom).** *The Oregon Trail.* Albert Bierstadt painted this picture in 1869 after having visited the West in 1859. **Page 15 (top).** *Map of the Oregon Trail.* Frémont's cartographer, Georg Carl Preuss, based this map on the field notes and journal of Captain John Charles Frémont. **Page 17.** *Thomas Hart Benton.* Mathew Brady's studio produced this daguerreotype of the senator from Missouri between 1845 and 1850.

WEB SITES

Due to the changing nature of Internet links, PowerKids Press has developed an online list of Web sites related to the subject of this book. This site is updated regularly. Please use this link to access the list:
www.powerkidslinks.com/feaw/jcfremnt/